Paul Cookson is not a villain, although he did once wait for a tortoise to reach the end of the garden and then turn it round.

He spends most of his time visiting schools, where he performs his poetry and helps pupils and staff to write their own poems. He also edits numerous poetry anthologies and performs regularly at festivals and libraries.

His favourite superhero is Batman (Adam West) and his favourite villain is Catwoman (Lee Meriwether) from the 1960s TV series – both looked good in tight-fitting suits.

Paul is married to Sally and they live in Retford with their children Sam and Daisy.

David Parkins is deeply villainous. He has one wife, six cats, three children (one of whom he forces to play the violin) and sings very loudly to annoy the neighbours. He spends most of his time drawing pictures.

And he has a beard! Ha Ha Ha Ha HAAAAH!

THE EVIL DOCTOR MUCUS SPLEEN

Villainous Poems chosen by

PAUL COOKSON

Illustrated by David Parkins

MACMILLAN CHILDREN'S BOOKS

Dedicated to the staff and pupils of the following primary schools: Bottesford, Croxton Kerrial, Harby, Hose, Long Clawson, Redmile, Stathern and Waltham – who all made the Vale of Belvoir Writing Project such good fun. Thanks!

First published 2001 by Macmillan Children's Books

This edition published 2011 by Macmillan Children's Books
a division of Macmillan Publishers Limited
20 New Wharf Road, London N1 9RR
Basingstoke and Oxford
Associated companies throughout the world
www.panmacmillan.com

ISBN 978-0-330-54589-1

3 5 7 9 8 6 4 2

A CIP catalogue record for this book is available from the British Library.

Printed and bound by CPI Group (UK) Ltd, Croydon, CR0 4YY

Contents

Cereal Killer

He marmalizes sugar puffs
He stabs his shredded wheat
He smothers his poor rice crispies
Yet none does Gnasher eat

He bashes up his porridge oats
Shouting, 'Death to polyfilla'
He always strikes at breakfast time
Does 'Gnash' the Cereal Killer.

Richard Caley

Villain of the Week

Monday's villain is foul of face,
Tuesday's villain has just eaten Grace,
Wednesday's villain gives loads of woe,
Thursday's villain brings ice and snow,
Friday's villain is creepy and scary,
Saturday's villain is smelly and hairy,
but the villain that's spawned on a Sunday morning,
does really nasty things – *without warning*!

Mike Johnson

Boo!
Sunday
Saturday
Thursday
Friday
Wednesday

Lex Loosener

When Lex Loosener leaps into town
His powers amaze and astound
He can make buttons melt
He will loosen your belt
And your trousers will fall to the ground.

Roger Stevens

Mother Christmas's Demand

Hear this, children of the world,
Father Christmas has cracked.
He's gone stark raving bonkers
and he won't be coming back.

And so, little kiddies, listen up,
from now on – you've got me.
That means NO MORE PRESENTS
under the Christmas tree.

I'm not driving that stupid sleigh
or jingling boring bells.
And you won't catch me squashing down chimneys,
or feeding reindeers. Anyway, they smell.

From now on – YOU MUST GIVE PRESENTS TO ME
Anyone who doesn't will die.
So don't be silly twits
or you'll get chopped into little bits
and baked into my next batch of mince pies.

P.S. All presents to be sent to: Mother Christmas,
Santa's Hut, Lapland.

Andrea Shavick

JINGLE
BELLS

The Teddy Bear Terrorists

We've got your best teddy,
if you want him back,
just put everything we demand
in a sack:
either we hear by Friday
or it's tough on Ted;
you'll get him back, slowly,
we'll start with the head.

Mike Johnson

The Secret of a Super Villain

He's a shirt-blowing
all-knowing
earth-quaking
nerve-shaking
cool-kissing
near-missing
fast-talking
never-walking
supersonic
near-bionic
spine-chilling
super villain!

But only before 8 o'clock as he's afraid of the dark.
After which he becomes a:

shirt-shrinking
cocoa-drinking
mummy-kissing
teddy-missing
thumb-sucking
problem-ducking
knee-knocking
baby-rocking
subsonic
near-chronic
unwilling
chicken villain.

Andrew Collett

The Evil Doctor Mucus Spleen

Who schemes an evil scheming scheme?
Who dreams an evil dreaming dream?
Who wants to rule the world supreme?
Who has the evillest inventions?
Who has the evillest intentions?
Thoughts and plans too dark to mention . . .
The Evil Evil Evil . . . Doctor Mucus Spleen!

Who's the crime at every scene?
Who wants to turn the whole world green?
Who's not ozone friendly-clean?
His phaser laser quasar blaster
Blasts his poison ever faster
Emerald phlegm in quick-dry plaster
The Evil Evil Evil . . . Doctor Mucus Spleen!

Whose operations and routines
Take science to the dark extremes?
Who's part alien, part machine?
His cauldrons bubble, test tubes fizz.
Sockets hum and wires whizz
I bet you know just who it is . . .
The Evil Evil Evil . . . Doctor Mucus Spleen!

Whose habits are the most obscene?
Whose toes are full of jam between?
Whose armpits boil and trousers steam?
Who drips slime and goo and ooze?
Who smells of ancient sweat-stained shoes?
Who's the baddest of bad news?
The Evil Evil Evil . . . Doctor Mucus Spleen!

PHLEGM

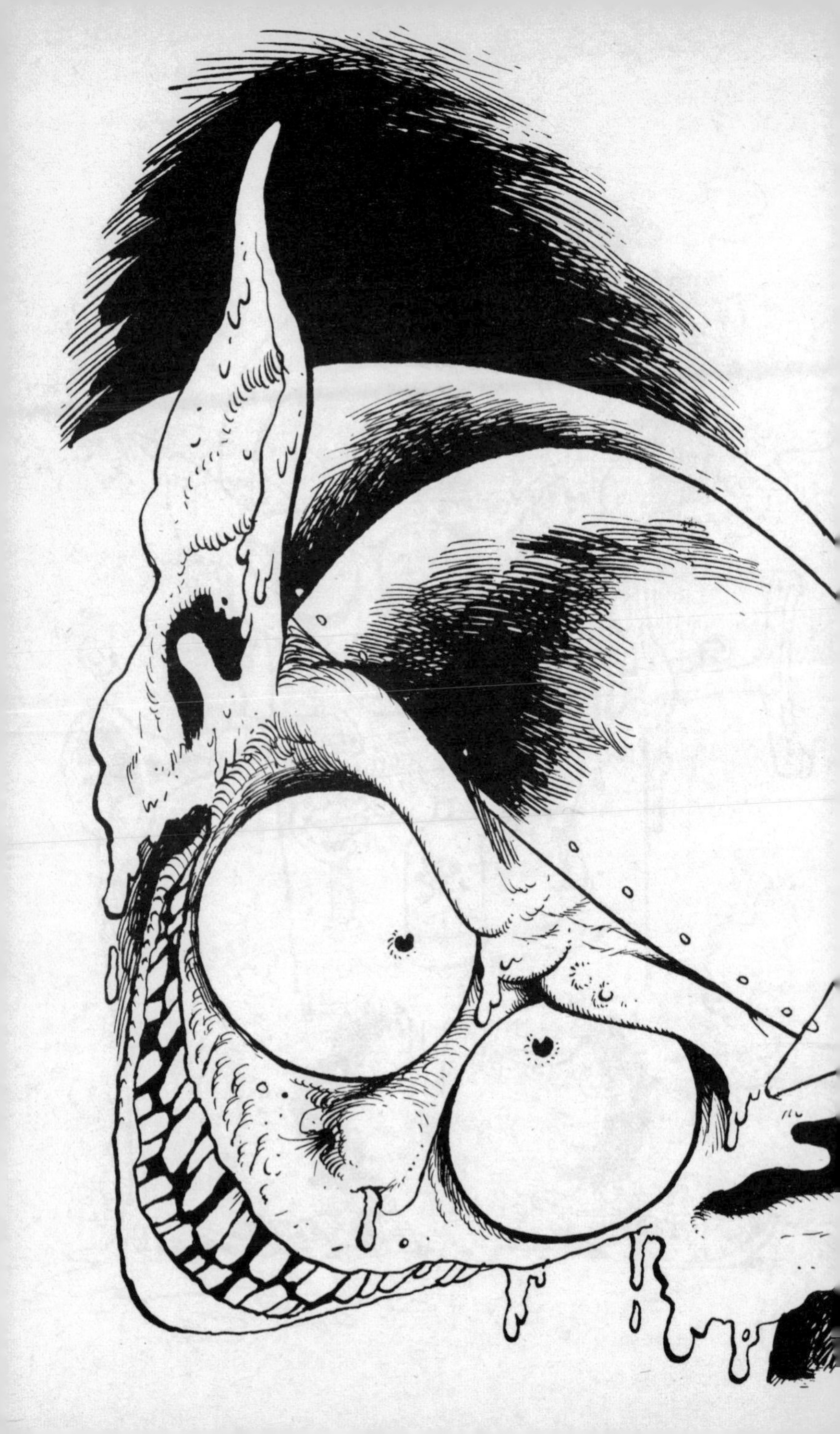

Whose underpants are trampolines?
Whose eyes are like two tangerines?
Whose skin's like rotten clotted cream?
Who has the stench of used baked beans?
Who makes your eyes and nostrils stream?
Who needs total quarantine?
The Evil Evil Evil . . . Doctor Mucus Spleen!

He's mean! He's green! He'll make you scream!
The baddest villain ever seen!
Watch out for his laser beam!
The Evil Evil Evil . . . Doctor Mucus Spleen!

Paul Cookson

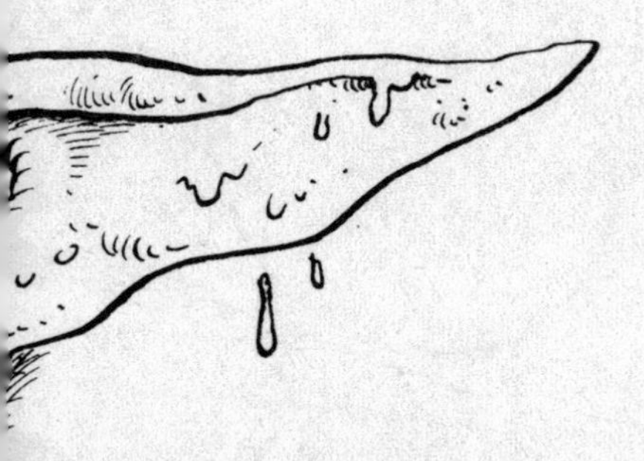

Last Friday Near the Shed

I was digging and I found a box.
I opened it and I found
an old red cape
a torn red mask
some mouldy red underpants
and a gun that shot red sauce.

So it was true.
My grandad really was
THE TOMATO.

All those years when he told us stories
about holding up the bus
and making all the passengers get off
just so that he could spray them with red sauce
he was telling the truth.

Imagine that.
My Grandad: THE TOMATO.

So I wonder if my grandma
really was
SQUID GIRL?

I'll get my spade.

Ian McMillan

The Sound Collector

A stranger called this morning
Dressed all in black and grey
Put every sound into a bag
And carried them away

The whistling of the kettle
The turning of the lock
The purring of the kitten
The ticking of the clock

The popping of the toaster
The crunching of the flakes
When you spread the marmalade
The scraping noise it makes

The hissing of the frying pan
The ticking of the grill
The bubbling of the bathtub
As it starts to fill

The drumming of the rain drops
On the window-pane
When you do the washing-up
The gurgle of the drain

The crying of the baby
The squeaking of the chair
The swishing of the curtain
The creaking of the stair

A stranger called this morning
He didn't leave his name
Left us only silence
Life will never be the same.

Roger McGough

The Wedding of Salmonella Toxin and Fungus Blight

It was a super villain's wedding. All the super villains came
(heroes not invited) the bride (her charming name
was Salmonella Toxin) wore a dress of poisonous green.
Among the super villains the undisputed queen,
she was marrying her sweetheart the revolting Fungus Blight,
that phosphorescent villain who glows biliously at night.
The bridesmaids were selected from the local women's jail.
All were tough and hairy and all were out on bail.
They carried little posies and their knuckledusters shone
and a hippo could have fitted in the dresses they had on.

The best man wore his costume, his notorious Ratman suit
and the presents piled up nicely, mostly bulging bags of loot.
Henchmen were the ushers and they cringed, with slimy grins
ushering the evil crowds of super villains in.
The couple were soon married. They both vowed eternal
fights
but Salmonella promised not to poison Fungus Blight.
An arch of super death rays was the Mad Professors' treat
and the pair emerged beneath them to the sharp, staccato
beat
of machine guns fired above them. As the bullets tinkled
down,
"They might have used confetti!" said the bridegroom with a
frown.

The wedding feast was sumptuous set out by the blushing
bride
and did awful things to super villains' sensitive insides.
Then Fungus spread some mould spores as the villains
writhed and groaned.
"We've been set up." Thin Konrad the Kleptomaniac moaned.
The happy couple made their getaway in style
knowing that their super chums were harmless for a while.
"Now the world is ours to dominate," said wily Salmonella
and snuggled up to Fungus Blight, her super villain fella.

Marian Swinger

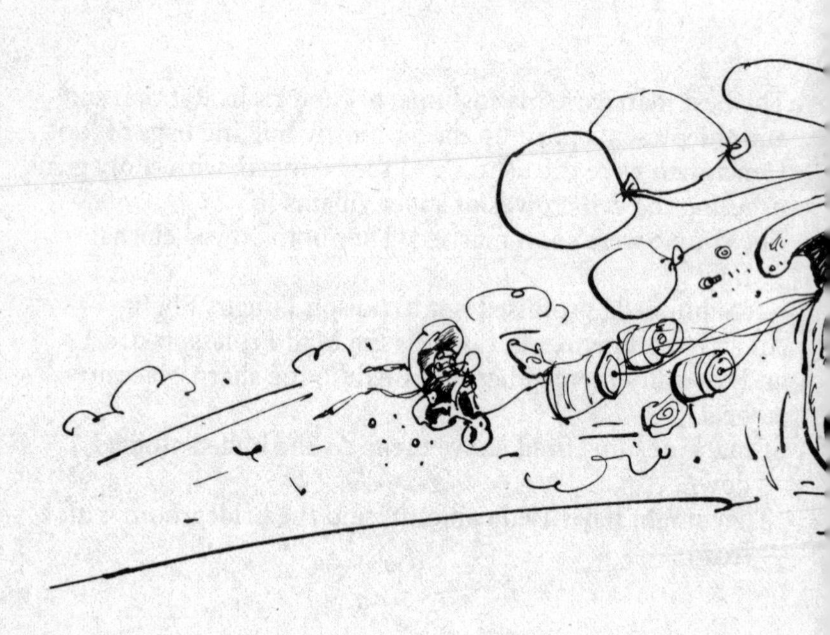

JUST MARRIED

Letter from a Super Villain's Mum

Dear World

I'm sorry that Walter (better known to you as *THE DARK LORD OF BLACKNESS, DESTROYER OF PURITY AND GOODNESS*) will not be able to rule you today as he is not feeling very well.

He has a runny nose and a temperature and is in bed with Teddy and a hot water bottle. (I did tell him to keep his vest on but does he ever take notice of his mum?!)

He has a sore throat . . . (too much evil laughing and sneering if you ask me).

The doctor says his asthma attacks may be due to an allergy to his giant white poodle *Titan* and has given him some tablets, which should help his wheezing.

With a bit of luck he should be back to making your life a misery next week – his tummy upset should have cleared up by then . . . (the toilet seat hasn't had a chance to get cold he's been on it that much . . .)

Anyway, if you could just pretend to be unhappy and downtrodden until Walter, sorry *THE DARK LORD OF BLACKNESS, DESTROYER OF PURITY AND GOODNESS* gets better that would be nice.

Yours faithfully,

Doreen Smith (Mrs)

Alias *CRUELLA MEDUSA GLOOM, MOTHER OF TERMINAL DOOM*

p.s. Meanwhile, step out of line and you'll have me to deal with!

Paul Cookson

Roll of Dishonour

Angry Alfred, the Assassin – axe, acid and 'andsaw artiste
Bold Brian, Birdbrain of the Bog, bully, braggart and beast

Charming Charlie who cheerfully chains up his chums in a cellar
Dirty Dora the dangerous dung-dumping dungeon dweller

Evil Eddie the egg-eating Educated Exterminator
Fat Francis the Flatulent, feared from Frankfurt to Fez and further

Ghastly Gertrude, the grim garrotting gran
Hideous Henry, the horrid hooded hang-gliding highwayman

Insolent Ian the Impatient Impaler who adds insult to injury
Gemstone Jeremy, jewel-thief and jester to the duped Duke of Germany

Comical Ken the Crooked Circus Killer – a song, a dance, a stab in the back
Loathsome Lady LardLips who looks like a lump of lead in a sack

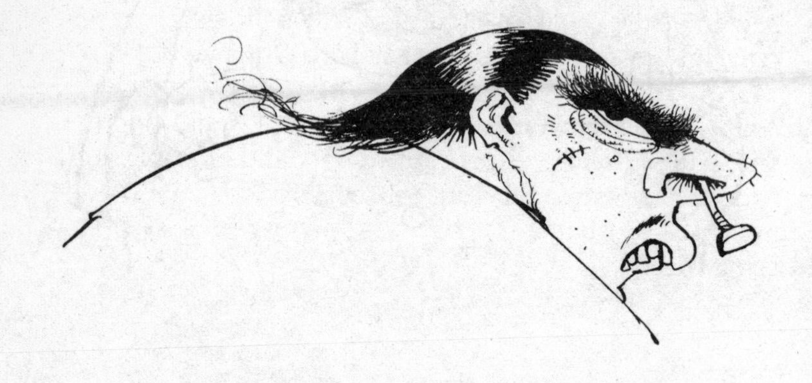

Mad Malkie, manic mass-murderer from the Mongolian mafia
Nail-Up-the-Nose Norman, not no-onè nastia

Oily Oliver of Aughton, awful oozing owl-disemboweller
Pongy Peter the particularly unpleasant pirate, pigfarmer and fowler

Queen Queechy the Quarrelsome, as queasy as an earthquake
Rude Randolf the Wretched, Rotten Robber of rubbish and ratcake

Simon the Slippery, second son of Septimus the Savage and
Sarah the SlySoandSo
Twitchy Thomas the Tired Thief of Thurso

Ugly Ulric the Undertaker, he's got a living to urn
Vengeful Violent Vera the Vurst Villains' Villian

Windy Walter the Warty, waif-whacker and wobbly blob
Xerxes the extremely expert executioner and excitable slob
Yucky Yolanda the Yabbering Yob
and at the very end
Zog the Zend.

Dave Calder

Ransom Note

I'm keeping Widow Twankey
Nice and cosy in a sack –
OH, YES I AM!
And if you want her back
Bring Aladdin's old lamp
(Inclusive of genie)
To the stage door at half past four.
Signed: The Panto Meanie

Sue Cowling

Dr Dastardly Doom and the Modish Mirror

Know, O Disciple of Doom, that villains are not as vain
as the glitter-suited Goodies who spoil our fun
and so I have invented this most interesting glass
which can be fitted in shop-windows, phone-boxes –
wherever a satin spangly superhero may appear
and need to quickly check his costume is correct.
One sideways glance will be enough to turn them into
victims of fashion –
their shiny swimsuits will sprout frills,
their tights will wrinkle and sag, their feet
will wobble on suddenly stacked heels and platform soles –

The fools will stare at it like this and . . .
Aargh!!

Dave Calder

A Bad Report

Alibiology: Unbelievable

Mafiamatics: Relatively poor

Meglamanery: Lacks ambition

Catastrophics: Disastrous

Plottery: Half-baked

Robgraphy: Holds everyone up

Fiendlish: Diabolical

Schemnastics: Must add more twists

Jane Clarke

Report.

My Kind of Villain

My kind of villain
is tall and thin
with a droopy moustache
that he strokes when vexed
or when considering
what kind of bad business
to get into next.
My kind of villain
in his hooded black cloak
plots wicked deeds
in a voice that's halfway
between cackle and croak,
dreams up fantastic schemes
and fiendish machines
but never succeeds:
though ruthless and strong
he's a bit of a joke –
something always goes wrong.
Dashing but dim,
doomed never to win –
that's my kind of villain

what's yours?

Dave Calder

Professor Venom's Academy for Super Villains

Timetable for Tuesday

9 a.m.	Assembly. Songs of Hate.
9.30 a.m.	Airborne superheroes. Identification from the ground. Bring silhouette charts.
10.30 a.m.	World Domination. How to become a dictator in ten easy goose steps.
11.15 a.m.	Break Do not destroy your enemies in the playground. It makes a nasty mess and puts an extra burden on Mr Sludge, your caretaker.
11.30 a.m.	Perfecting the fiendish cackle. You will not achieve your super villain's diploma until you have mastered this.
12 midday	Disabling your superhero. Bring your own Krypton. Rare and undetectable poisons for which there is no known antidote will be supplied by the Academy.

1 p.m.	Dinner Any student caught slipping rare and undetectable poisons for which there is no known antidote into their neighbour's Coke will be excluded. There has been too much of this lately.
2 p.m.	Mad Science Do it yourself Death Rays. Kits available at any good hardware store. Make sure they are European Safety Standard approved.
3 p.m.	Football. The Art of the Foul. Don't forget the match against Dr Do-Good's School for Superheroes is coming up soon so you will want to pay particular attention to this lesson.
4 p.m.	Home time. Once again we implore parents not to vaporise the traffic wardens. You must expect to be booked if you park your assault vehicles on the zig zag lines outside the Academy.

Marian Swinger

The Mad Magician

In a dark and dingy dungeon
The Mad Magician dwells,
Mixing poisonous potions,
Concocting evil spells.

Into his bubbling cauldron
The Mad Magician throws
Handfuls of wriggling maggots,
The eyes of two dead crows,

The bladder of a nanny goat,
The snout of a year-old pig,
An eagle's claw, a vampire's tooth,
Hairs plucked from a judge's wig.

He waves his wicked wizard's wand.
He utters a piercing cry.
From their lairs, deep in the earth,
A thousand demons fly.

In a dark and dingy dungeon
The Mad Magician dwells,
Mixing poisonous potions,
Concocting evil spells.

John Foster

Bad Eggs

Welcome to the action committee
of the truly hard-boiled.
Our mission, as our founder said,
is to "Make a mess and create a fuss!"
His martyrdom through "the accident"
when pushed off a wall will be
forever remembered.
Others also are sadly missed owing to
mishaps with electric cookers.
A minute's silence, please,
for those who have fried.
Some less worthy members have been poached
by those sunny side up do-gooders
who are ova the moon
when conversions are made.

Have patience my cracked and addled friends
revenge will be ours.
Such a stink shall we raise
that folks will name us
"the first of the phew!"
Chickens will be made to realize
who came first.
Our beloved Humpty Dumpty
had no fear of military might
as soldiers proved useless.

We have signed a pact
with demonstrators everywhere
to stand high and be ready to hand.
Keep the faith, ovoids. When the order comes –
SCRAMBLE!

John C. Desmond

5 Villains

I know who
pushed
Pussy down the well.
(ding-dong)

And who
pushed
Humpty off the wall
(spitter spatter)

I know who
tripped
Jack coming down the hill
(Ahhhh!)

I also know
who shot the sparrow
who shot Cock Robin

And who put
five and twenty blackbirds
in the king's pie.

But I'm not telling.

I'll just give a clue.

Retep Noxid

Evil titter!

Henchman Wanted . . .

Must have mountains of muscle and not much brain
Must have loyalty beyond the call of pain
Must have hairy tattooed knuckles that reach the floor
And a head that's flat that can smash through any door.

Must have a cheerful obedient disposition
Must volunteer for every life-threatening suicide mission
Must be able to carry all the Master's equipment, no matter how big and strong
Must be able to take the blame when all the plans to rule the world go wrong.

Must be able to fight to the death while the Master gets away
Must be able to work without sleeping twenty-four hours every single day.
Must be able to groom and tend to every whim of his favourite pet, wherever sent
Must never, ever get paid – not even a single compliment.

Must be able to wash and cook, clean, iron, run the Master's bath
Must not get tired of the Master's evil annoying hideous laugh
And finally, but by no means leastly
Must always bring the Master his milky coffee and fairy cake on time,

No matter how much the Master is beastly.

Paul Cookson

CUDDLES
LOVE

The Evil Genius

Don't look around,
keep your eyes on the page,
act as naturally as you can.
You just need to know, before you read on,
that you're being watched by *The Evil Genius.*

What – you've never heard of *The Evil Genius,*
that genius whose mission is to tease and frustrate
for nothing more than riches and a bit of a fiendish cackle?

Well, you know how
when you try to open a crisp packet,
how you pick and pick
and nibble and pick until, finally,
you tug *so* hard
that the whole bag suddenly rips apart
in a great explosion of crisps?
(Snigger, snigger)
Well, guess who invented the crisp packet?

And you know what happens
whenever you try to use a nut cracker?
(Snigger, snigger)
Well, guess who created the nut cracker . . .
And antiseptic cream – and sticking plasters too?

And yesterday when you tried to put up that deckchair . . .
(Snigger, snigger)
what a classic!
Do I need to tell you who invented the deckchair . . .
not to mention plaster of Paris?
(Snigger, snigger)

So who am I?
I'm *The Evil Genius'* sniggering sidekick *Clever Dick.*
And why am I telling you all this?
Because there's nothing funnier than *that* look
on a victim's face
(Snigger, snigger)
when they find out they've been set up.
(Ha Ha Ha Ha Ha Ha)

Philip Waddell

King JB

We have implanted
our subject jellybabies
with micro chips,
programming them
to rise up and march
on all town halls,
railway stations and banks.
Some will penetrate the Internet
and gum up computers.
Too long have we suffered
at the hands of humans;
brutal beheadings,
torn limb from limb
and the drawn-out torture
of being sucked to death.
Enough is enough.
Passive resistance has failed;
our cries ignored.
Time for us to throw a wobbly.
Sticky wickets, traffic jams,
glue ears, bogged downs
will pale into insignificance
before the might of our forces.
Tremble all ye of the sweet tooth!

John C. Desmond

Dr D. Rision's Shopping List

scornflakes
laughing stock cubes
sour grapes
caustic soda
scathing pads
marshmalice
acid drops
throat sweets (honey and venom)
spite bulbs (40 watt)
ginger jeer
teasebags
Taunton cider
mock turtle soup
fault and pepper
Cornish nasty
crabby paste
carp
I Can't Believe it's not Bitter!
1 packet choccy takethemickeys
baked spleens
bread (Mother's Snide)
disdain remover
scoff for dinner party
gripe water.

Sue Cowling

Principal Crook

I found whilst sorting library books,
the *I Spy Book of Master Crooks.*
One 'undercover crook' selects
the sort of jobs no one suspects,
despite his being very scary –
his teeth are metal, limbs are hairy,
his eyes are cold, expression evil,
his knuckles trail, and 'looks' primeval.
He prowls around with sneers and growls,
he's patchy stubble over jowls –
he has no neck (like a gorilla),
his breath makes a good insect killer.
He likes no one, and there's a rumour,
he's no heart or sense of humour –
And I've realized this ghastly creature
is Mr Grimm, our new headteacher!

Liz Brownlee

I-SPY
BOOK OF
MASTER
CROOKS

Vocabulary for Villains

Fiendish, fearsome, filthy,
Revolting, rancid, vicious;
Detestable, disgusting,
Malevolent, malicious.

Ghastly, grisly, gruesome,
Menacing, atrocious;
Grim, grotesque, repulsive,
Loathsome, foul, ferocious.

Hellish, diabolical,
Hateful, hideous, mean;
Odious, malodorous,
Venomous, unclean.

Wicked, evil, ugly, vile,
Callous, cruel, spiteful;
Horrific, harsh, horrendous,
Pitiless and frightful.

I've given you the adjectives;
Now it's your turn to be clever:
Go ahead, enjoy it,
Write the vilest poem ever.

Eric Finney

A BAD REPORT

Alibiology: Unbelievable

Mafiamatics: Relatively poor

Meglamanery: Lacks ambition

Catastrophics: Disastrous

Plottery: Half-baked

Robgraphy: Holds everyone up

Fiendlish: Diabolical

Schemnastics: Must add more twists

Jane Clarke

Cover illustration by Martin Chatterton

ISBN 978-0-330-54589-1

UK £3.99

www.panmacmillan.com